Learn to build
Interpersonal Skills

N Chokkan

Learn to build Interpersonal Skills
© *New Horizon Media*

First Edition: March 2010
64 Pages
Printed in India.

ISBN 978-81-8493-431-1
Pro-ya-en-73

Prodigy Books
177/103, First Floor, Ambal's Building
Lloyds Road, Royapettah, Chennai 600 014.
Ph: +91-44-4200-9603
Email: support@nhm.in
Website: www.nhm.in

Prodigy Books is an imprint of New Horizon Media Pvt. Ltd.

The World Health Organization has defined life skills as, 'the abilities for adaptive and positive behaviour that enable individuals to deal effectively with the demands and challenges of everyday life.'

Life skills are essentially those abilities that help promote mental well-being and competence in young people as they face the realities of life. With life skills, one is able to explore alternatives, and understand one's strengths and weaknesses.

Interpersonal Relationship is one of the ten core life skill strategies and techniques listed by WHO (World Health Organisation)

List of core life skill strategies and techniques listed by WHO

Effective communication

Creative thinking

Decision-making

Problem solving

Critical thinking

Interpersonal relationship skills

Self-awareness

Empathy

Coping with emotions

Coping with stress

No Islands Here

Yesterday was a very special day for me.

Two of my friends were celebrating their birthdays, and guess what – both of them invited me to their parties.

But when I went to the parties, I was surprised by the contrast. One of them had lots and lots of people, and the other one was practically deserted.

After the long day, I started thinking about it. Two persons, celebrating their birthdays on the same day, had invited almost the same set of people… While one of them had guests pouring in, the other got a very lukewarm response. Why? What could be the reason?

It did not warrant too much of thought; I could get the answer almost immediately.

My first friend is a social darling. He likes people and they like him too. Whenever he is around, you can see smiling faces, hear loud laughter and the whole world will be a better place to live.

On the other hand, my second friend is a loner. He likes doing things on his own, doesn't believe in involving others in whatever he is up to. Basically, he thinks only about himself and not others. His strange behaviour has isolated him from the society, and earned him very few (if not zero) friends.

Of course, I don't mean to say the second friend is a bad person. He is a fantastic thinker, hard worker and everyone who meets him has something to admire about him. But when it comes to interpersonal relationship skills, he lacks it badly. That's why his birthday party had very few takers.

What is interpersonal relationship? Is it very important?

The answers are quite obvious, as you can see from the above example.

We can't live all alone in this world. At any given point of time, there are people around us – parents, brothers, sisters, other relatives, friends, teachers and colleagues and many others. We regularly talk to these people, interact with them, and mutually support each other. This is what we call interpersonal relationship.

To summarise, it is the ability to establish and maintain relationships with others in the society. It helps us a great deal in our daily interactions and gives us a positive guiding force.

Let us look at a practical example to understand the importance of this. We all know that the earth is spherical in shape. But what kind of sphere it is? Can you guess?

Something like a Cricket ball? A laddu?

No. The earth's inner area (or the core) may be perfectly spherical and strong. But its surface (the area where we live) is nothing but a collection of plates. Imagine lots of papers spread out next to each other, and few piled up — the earth's surface is made of plates arranged in such a manner. But the earth doesn't look like that. It's a perfect solid to our eyes.

True. We are not able to see the layers of the earth because the plates are huge. But they do exist, and scientists have conducted numerous experiments and proved that they are there.

Now, the earthen sheets should have a good relationship with the surrounding layers or plates. Otherwise, they may move and hit the nearby sheets and cause earthquakes and other disasters.

The same logic can be applied in our life. Just like the earth's sheets that exist in harmony, we need to maintain a good relationship with people around us. Instead, if we create conflicts, we may have to face earth-shaking problems everyday.

There are many kinds of interpersonal relationships that we encounter everyday. Some of them are:

- Family (mother, father, siblings, grand parents and other relatives)

- Friends (classmates, neighbourhood friends, even a few strangers and acquaintances)

- Social contacts (people who may not be your close friends but with whom you interact on a regular basis). For example, the person who drives your school bus, security guard of your apartment, the temple priest, your friends' parents, the doctor who treats you and so on)

- Acquaintances at Work/School (As a kid, you interact with your school teachers, dance master, yoga guruji and so on, who come under this category. Your father or mother will also have similar contacts with their colleagues and business partners).

- Others (people who don't fall under any of the above four categories)

If you observe these categories carefully, we spend more time with these people (who form our social network) than with anyone else. This warrants that some special attention be paid in improving our relationships with them.

But what do we gain by that? First, anybody maintaining a healthy relationship with others gets equally strong support and guidance from everyone. This helps them to get ahead faster than others who live isolated like islands.

For example, if you have too many friends, it automatically boosts your self confidence among your peers. You want to excel in whatever you do to earn their respect, and if something goes wrong, you know your friends will be there to support you. This positive energy keeps you physically and mentally agile and helps in everything you do.

On the other hand, think of people with poor interpersonal relationship skills. Even if they succeed in their endeavours, they have no one to share it with and this makes them lose motivation in getting ahead in studies, or anything in life. It will be a dull life, isn't it?

I am sure you don't want to belong to the second category. In the next few chapters, let us learn the art of building and maintaining relationships with everyone around us. After that, the whole world will become our friends!

'Borrow'yana

In my school days, I had a friend whom my friends and I called 'Borrowyana'. His real name was Narayana but we had to call him by this name because he always borrowed something or the other from everyone around. For example, he would forget to bring graph sheets to Mathematics class. When the teacher arrives, he would go around asking each one of us to spare one sheet.

For us, giving him one sheet was not a problem. So, we helped our friend. He collected many such sheets and managed the class. Next would be History class, for which he would have forgotten to bring the map. Again, he would ask everyone, 'Anyone got an extra map?' During lunch time, he would finish his food very fast, and then sit with all the others sampling each one's lunch and savouring it.

As we were school kids, we didn't mind Borrowyana's ways. After all, he was our friend and we liked helping him. Sometimes, we did tease him, but just for fun.

Now, when I look back and reminisce, I perceive a very important lesson from these incidents. Any relationship has to be a two-way lane with an equal give and take. Otherwise, at some point of time or the other, there will be conflicts.

You would have heard of business partnerships. Two or more people come together and start a company. One of them organises the funds, the second brings in the expertise, and the third connects the new company to a lot of potential customers, while the fourth works hard on the field.

Now, because each of them has brought something to the table, we can assume their relationships are going to be good. But at the end of the year, whatever be the profits, they are shared among the partners as per the original agreement, because all of them have contributed to the company in some way or the other.

Let us assume that there is a fifth partner who doesn't do anything for the company. He has no money, no skills, and no social contacts, and is not ready to work either. Just because he is a good friend of the other four partners, they agreed to make him a partner.

Initially, this arrangement may work because all of them are friends. They wouldn't mind helping the fifth partner, who is a modified version of our dear old Borrowyana. But after sometime, this relationship is bound to sour. One person or the other may start thinking, 'What did he do for the company? Why is he enjoying all the benefits when he has put in no effort and we do all the hard work?'

So, whatever be the relationship, you have to remember it as a two way lane – what (or how much) you are bringing to the table is very important.

Take any of your school friends as an example. You may be studying together or playing in the same team. Sometimes, you would be teaching your friend a complex mathematics problem, and the next day he might take you to fishing and teach you how to master that art. Indirectly, you are both contributing to the relationship in some way or the other.

This doesn't mean that every time you do something you should expect something in return. On a bigger scheme of things, you have to be careful in making sure that all the parties involved in a relationship is contributing to it, constantly.

The key point here is, when you are in a relationship with your friend, brother, sister, teacher, whoever it may be, avoid being selfish. No one likes that.

Similarly, sharing is essential for relationships. It may be sharing your books, toys or knowledge and skills. Sometimes it may be just listening to them and sharing their happiness, worries and other feelings. This is the main reason people look for relationships.

Interpersonal relationships thrive on complete sharing, of responsibilities and results. For example, tomorrow there is a kids' carnival in school. You and your friend decide to put up a small sweetmeat stall there. So how would you share responsibilities and results?

One way is, sharing the investment (money) required. Both of you may count your pocket money and decide how much you can invest on buying sweets. And what if one of you has no savings? In that case, the person can't contribute. But the person can take care of other responsibilities such as decorating the stall, making advertisement banners, calling out to people to come to your stall.

Once you have shared your responsibilities like this, the project will go on smoothly. There won't be a question of Borrowyanas here, because each one is contributing to it. This leads us to the next question, of sharing the results and benefits. At the end of the day, suppose your sweet stall has made a profit of Rs. 100. Both of you having contributed to the stall's success by sharing responsibilities, you can happily split this amount, without any misunderstanding or conflict.

Sharing is a wonderful feeling which brings everyone closer to you. In fact, you can try it with anyone. Next time you see a new boy or girl in your neighborhood try welcoming the newcomer with a candy or an ice cream. It works like magic and gets you lots and lots of friends.

Here, what you share is not important. But the very attitude that you are ready to share, makes you a special person, which attracts others towards you and helps you maintain healthy relationships. Once you have a good set of friends (or in other types of relationships), you can't take them for granted. There are few important aspects to be considered to maintain these relationships.

First, be flexible. If you are rigid and not ready to change for others, they would start thinking 'why should I hang out with this guy?' For example, you are going to your schoolmate's house. It's a hot day, and they don't have an air conditioner at home. What would you do?

You may have an air conditioner at home that functions throughout the day. But for your friend's sake, you decide not to complain about it and concentrate on having fun, or studying. Such small adjustments are critical in enhancing relationships.

Next, relationships shouldn't be created out of fear. They should evolve naturally; otherwise they will break, sooner or later. Imagine you have a school bully. Whenever people see him, they salute, smile, laugh at his jokes, and give him snacks, sweets, money, and everything they have in their pocket. Does this mean the school bully is a master of interpersonal relationships?

No. The same people, who are praising him now, will turn away from him at the first opportunity they get. Relationships can never be forced on people. That's where the concept of sharing and mutual support comes into picture. You don't have to look for a benefit every time you interact with people, but all the people in a relationship should sincerely feel the need of others, and genuinely enjoy the company. This bond is very difficult to achieve. But once you have it, it's a priceless possession and you would enjoy the relationship unfolding to greater levels!

Hear vs Listen

When others talk, what do you do? Hear? Or Listen? These two words may sound similar. But in reality they are very much different. When you hear someone talk, all you need is your two ears. Whatever they say enters your head via one ear and exits through the other. Nothing stays in between.

This is what we do during a boring lecture in a classroom. The teacher may be talking about many things, but we don't grasp anything. However, when the same teacher talks about something interesting, a subject you love, you not only hear but listen. In other words, you digest whatever the teacher says, extract the important points and register them in your brain. All these processes need full concentration, and much greater effort than simple hearing.

Now, think of it from another angle. You are talking to one of your friends. Do you want them to simply hear you, or listen to you?

Of course, we want them to listen to us. If they don't, we feel they are insulting us.

The same is true on the other side of the table. When you want to maintain healthy relationships with people around you, one of the top skills you need to acquire is listening!

It's not as difficult as it sounds. All you need to do is, concentrate fully on what the other person is saying. If you don't understand something, make a mental note of it and ask for clarifications later. That gives the person a feeling that you respect him or her.

Some people just can't listen to others. They always want to talk, and interrupt others constantly. This is a nasty habit and a proven relationship killer. For example, listen to this conversation:

'Hey, guess what… we went to Goa for the Christmas vacation. We visited many wonderful beaches and …'

'Goa is great. I have visited it two years back. Unfortunately, it was raining at that time and we had to stay indoors. My dad taught us some very interesting indoor games and blah blah blah blah …'

Now imagine how the first person would feel. Forget listening, the second person didn't even let him talk. How will this relationship thrive, when the very basic ingredient of a healthy conversation is missing?

Similarly, some people have another irritating habit... jumping to conclusions, or saying things like 'I know'. For example, 'Today I was stopped by the policeman when I was crossing the road and ...'

'I know, he warned you for walking carelessly on the road, right?'

'No. He asked the time, as he forgot to wear his watch today.'

In this case, the second friend not only interrupted the first one's talk, he jumped into conclusion too soon and started with an 'I know'. In fact, he didn't know what happened. Even if he knew, it's humane to let others talk, allow them to say what's in their mind and then give our opinion(s) on the subject.

Many times, we assume people talk to us because we are superior. So when they talk about some problem they have faced, we immediately interrupt them, correct them, and offer our advice or suggestions.

The fact is that they don't need our solutions. If they needed, they would ask for it explicitly. Like, 'What do you think about this?' or 'What do you suggest I do about this?'

When others are not asking like that, it is better we just listen to them. Many times, they may just want to talk. If you listen to what they are saying with complete concentration, that itself will be a huge relief for them.

Also, it is not a good habit for us to judge people based on what they say. In such scenarios, we need to have an open mind and avoid making comments like, 'That's a very nasty thing you did.'

This doesn't mean you shouldn't talk at all. In a forthcoming chapter, we shall discuss in detail about the talking part. For the moment, let us just listen, and believe me, it will improve your relationships than any other tips you learn from this book!

Another important thing to remember is that when others are talking, constantly give them a suggestion that you are listening to them. It may be a simple nod of head every few minutes, or small statements like 'Oh', 'I see', 'Interesting' etc. These tiny gestures go a long way in terms of improving your friend's confidence and morale.

Finally, after they have finished speaking, you can summarise the gist of their talk. If they ask for it, provide your opinions or suggestions. Otherwise, simply acknowledge their feelings and they would love you for that!

Hierarchy of Needs

It's a summer holiday. You are being a good boy helping your mother clean-up the attic.

Now, there is a curious looking lamp there. You just take it out and rub it to clean.

The next minute, a genie pops out of the lamp and says, 'Hello boss, how are you?'

You know how this works. You have three wishes to ask; the genie will grant you those wishes and vanish forever. In such a situation, what are the three things you would wish for?

Let us pause for a moment here. Assume that the same thing happened to your brother or sister, or the boy next door. Do you think you will all wish for the same three things?

No. You may wish for a bicycle, which your sister may not want. She would like to have a nice new book instead. But your neighbour may want an endless supply of chocolates. So, just like people differ, their needs are also different. This understanding will help you a lot when cultivating interpersonal relationships.

There is a fantastic theory which describes this. It is called Maslow's hierarchy of needs. Abraham Maslow, an American psychologist introduced this theory in 1943, where he explained five distinct levels in which human needs work. Those five levels are:

- Physiological Needs

- Safety Needs

- Love/Belonging Needs

- Esteem Needs

- Self-Actualisation Needs

A person may start from the very base of this hierarchy. For example, a baby will have only physiological needs, it has to breathe regularly, whenever it's hungry, it needs food, water, good amount of sleep etc.

Once these physiological needs are met, people go to the next level, where they look for safety. This may include making sure that our body is not hurt while playing, and having our family members or friends around us whenever we need.

In the next level, we have the needs of a sense of belonging. This is where friendship comes into picture. People want to meet interesting personalities, and have various kinds of relationships with them. The last two are advanced levels in which people looking for respect in the society, and self-actualisation by creating something or leaving a legacy in the society are included.

Studying this hierarchy of needs is essential in making human relationships work. Because, when you understand others' needs, you have made the all-important first impression already. If you show them care, fulfil their needs and act accordingly, people are automatically drawn towards you. For example, when someone is hungry, you can't go to them and praise them saying, 'You are a great friend, I like hanging around with you'. He will simply say, 'All that is fine, but I can't eat that praise.'

The common mistake that many young friends make in a relationship is they assume that others think like them, and they have similar (or same) needs. This is not true; it can't be – we all are born different and our thought process is also different. If we understand this and start looking at things from a third person's perspective, our approach to people will be totally different.

The trick is to simply understand others' needs and respect their feelings, and change our behaviour accordingly. This small change will make us handle relationships more efficiently. We should not act in a similar way with everyone, but customise our behaviour according to their needs.

Consider the following scenarios. Which level of need do you think these people are in? To connect with them, what kind of approach will work?

- A boy has lost his pen. He is crying because his father will beat him up if he comes to know about this.

- A girl booked a ticket for a music concert. Excited about watching her favourite musician play live, she told her friends about it. But unexpectedly, the program got cancelled at the last minute. This makes her disappointed and dejected.

- A person is a total stranger to you. But you are forced to spend 10 hours with him in a train. He is talking to someone over the phone, 'I am meeting my mother and father after two months. I'm very excited.'

- She is trying to draw a picture. But something isn't right; so she paints something and throws it away in disappointment. She is on the verge of breaking down.

In addition to hierarchy of needs, another relationship factor we may consider is, 'Self Control Scale.' You might have noticed—some people show emotions openly, while others hide them. Not that they do it willingly, but by nature they are not very open and are able to control their emotions instead of expressing them.

Consider this example. Exam results are announced, and two children pass out with 97% marks. One of them is excited and goes around the block distributing sweets and crackers, whereas the other one silently goes home and tells his parents about it, without any emotions.

This doesn't mean that the second child doesn't like winning, or is unhappy. Sure, he enjoys the score he has achieved, but doesn't express it openly. Such persons prefer that others also behave the same way with them.

In the above example, the first child would love if someone patted him on the back and said, 'Great job buddy!' But the second child would prefer a handshake and a formal 'Congratulations'. So, before deciding how to build relationship with others, closely observe them, and you will get your clue!

I, Me, Myself

Two scholars met at a conference. One person started talking about his work, achievements, the praise he has received from others, awards he has won and so on. After five minutes, the other scholar got visibly upset. But this fellow didn't stop. He continued for about half an hour and then finally stopped.

'Thank god, you stopped talking about yourself,' said the second scholar sarcastically.

'Oh yes' the first one said, smiling proudly, 'I need to give a chance to you too, to talk about me.'

I guess this anecdote would have given you a clear idea about Ego.

If you look at the dictionary definition of Ego, it's self-image, thinking about ourselves. There is nothing wrong in thinking about oneself. But if we think

ONLY about our side of the story, we neglect everyone around us and that causes a serious relationship problem.

But how to overcome this?

There is a simple exercise or experiment which you can use for this purpose. It's called the "You test."

It's very simple. When you meet others, just observe them carefully, how many minutes it takes for them to use the word 'you' for the first time. Some people just boast about themselves, they may take so much time to even realise that you are in front of them. Others take one or two ice-breaker sentences and quickly start using the magic word, 'you'.

You can see that the more 'you's the person uses, the more we like them. The reverse is also true.

So, the simple trick is, when talking to people, use the 'you' word as soon as possible. This will give you a chance to understand their perspective and avoid falling into the Ego trap.

In the West, many young people are trained to use this "you test" to identify their true friends, classmates, hostel buddies, and even to choose their husband or wife. Talking about the other person matters a lot, if you want to move ahead in relationships of any sort.

To enhance this further, we need to build a special skill which is called broad vision. This would help us to see things from a distance, and include something more than just us. Even though it sounds difficult, mastering broad vision is not a tough task. All you need to learn is a different thought process.

Let us say you are standing in a room, you can only see people around you. Instead, if you are on a stage, you can see many people. Similarly, before you work on anything, start seeing it from a distance. Now you can observe that there may be more than one person (you) in the story.

Let us imagine that you are preparing for an important examination. Instead of doing everything on your own, you may think of asking help from your father to teach you some complex algebra, ask mother to tell you easy ways to remember the historical incidents and years, ask your close friend to train you on plotting cities in a map and so on.

Now, who gets the benefit of all these? You. But what happens in the process? You build a strong relationship with many people – your parents, brothers, sisters, friends, or even strangers.

Of course, you could have achieved the same without the help of others. But where is the fun? As long as there are mutual benefits, everyone would love to help you, and will only like you more! Remember, the reverse should also be true. Tomorrow if they approach you for help, your Ego may stop you from supporting them. It will make you say things like 'Today I am very tired, I need some rest, I can't help him with his homework.'

Don't say these aloud because they are definitely relationship breakers. No one likes selfish people who think only about themselves! Does this mean you have to sacrifice your own time and energy to help others? Not really. But try to be accommodative, and avoid Ego which may hurt your broad vision.

Everyone has to remember one thing – you may be great, I may be great, but when a healthy relationship binds the two of us, the sum of our energies will be much greater. In other words, as a team, 'we' will be able to do many things that we couldn't have achieved individually. To make this happen, we need to remove the Villain called Ego!

Curse of Knowledge

Few years back, researchers experimented with a group of people. To start with, they split the people into two teams. The first team was called 'Tappers' and the second 'Listeners'. Very curious names indeed!

They asked a person in the first team to come forward, and secretly told him the name of a famous song – It may be a nursery rhyme like "Rain Rain Go Away," or a pop song, or even a television jingle. This person has to tap the song on a table. The listeners group has to carefully listen to this tapping and identify the song. Sounds so easy, doesn't it?

No. Even though the songs chosen were popular, more than 90% of the listeners couldn't identify the songs.

They just drew a blank, confused as to what the other person was tapping. This made the tappers restless, and they started saying things like, 'Come on, I am tapping the tune clearly, why can't you identify?'

Their frustration is understandable. But at the same time, they were missing a very important lesson – it's called the Curse of Knowledge!

In the above example, the tappers already knew what the song was. Because of that, they could easily tap whatever was playing in their mind. That's why they feel that others will also recognize the song, because it's so obvious to them.

Now take a look from the other side, the listeners group has no knowledge of the song. It could be any of the millions of songs. So they are forced to think of so many options. This makes the tappers disappointed, 'It's so clear; why can't you identify it?'

This is called the Curse of Knowledge. Because they know it already, they are not able to understand the feeling of not knowing it. So, they naturally assume that the listeners are stupid.

We make the same mistake in our real life relationships too. We assume other people are of our wavelength and talk to them. If they don't understand we blame them, without even thinking once that the mistake could be on our side too. To overcome this, we need to learn to reach the other person's level and change the way we communicate.

Consider this case. Two boys are trying to be part of the school cricket team. One of them has been trained by his own father, and has already learnt the important skills that a cricketer needs. But the other person is a novice and he hopes to learn from the school team's experience, if selected.

The first boy looks at the other boy playing and comments, 'That's not cricket, you are just hitting the ball hard and running, you have no technique at all, your game sucks.' This may be a correct observation. But think of the impact it will make on the boys' relationship.

Instead, in the same situation, the first boy could have said, 'You are very powerful, your shots really make the ball disappear outside the stadium, I wish I could do it', and then carefully add, 'To improve your skills further, you may have to learn a few finer techniques of the game, and that will make you a great cricketer.'

Basically, both the statements convey the same message. But in the second case, the trained boy talks with understanding and empathy, keeping in mind that the other boy is a novice. This will make their relationship stronger.

Another example could be your teachers. All of them are much elder to you, and know many things which you don't. But do they show off their 'knowledge' when they talk to you?

Well, some teachers may do it. But good teachers always interact with the students at their level and explain things in their language, in a manner they can understand. This is what makes them more efficient and lovable.

You can observe the same in books too. Authors know the subject very well. But if they have curse of knowledge, they can't even imagine how readers (like us) would feel. Great writers overcome this bottleneck, learn to understand the readers' mind, and explain things in a way that is easily absorbed by the reader.

When you do this, another magic will happen. Those who are at a level below you in knowledge on the subject will be able to catch on with your help. Slowly, you will reach a stage where both of you will be able to communicate more effectively. Building such a relationship needs lot of patience. Once established, it will be very much rewarding and everlasting!

It's a Two Way Street!

One day, Mohan was coming back from school. He doesn't commute by school bus because his home is nearby. It's just a ten minutes' walk through a crowded street. Suddenly, it started raining. Mohan ran for shelter in a corner shop.

Then he started thinking, 'Why wait here unnecessarily? If I run fast, I can reach home in two or three minutes.' So he started running. In the next few minutes, he got drenched. He did reach home fast and dry himself. But the rain had its effect on him, he was down with cold and fever the next day.

As the news about Mohan's fever spread, his friends came to meet him. Most of them were very sympathetic;

they gave him a 'Get Well Soon' card and promised to share class notes with him, so that he doesn't miss any of his lessons due to illness.

But Rishi, one of Mohan's close friends found this incident funny. He started advising Mohan, 'What did you think? Don't you know it's dangerous to get wet in the pouring rain? This is all your fault; you should have waited at that shop till the rain stopped.'

Rishi is 100% right. But does it do any good for Mohan? Can he go back in time and change whatever has happened? No. Then what is the point in highlighting that mistake and advising him?

Soon, Mohan started hating Rishi and their relationship went for a toss. The fact is, people don't like to listen to advice. Whether it comes from parents, teachers, friends, siblings, it doesn't matter. But they don't like others telling them what they should do, or worse, what they should have done.

Does this mean that we should turn a blind eye to whatever people do? Should we remain silent even if they make a terrible mistake? Of course not. At the same time, we have to be careful in making it sound like a mutually arrived at decision, instead of giving advice. Then it won't be seen by people as a bad thing, or they won't consider you a 'big mouth'.

On the same day Mohan fell ill, his father took him to a hospital. While they were waiting for the doctor to arrive, Mohan's father started discussing with him, 'You must be feeling very bad, covered in these sweaters and mufflers, and not being able to go out and play with your friends, isn't it?'

'Yes dad,' Mohan's voice was filled with pain, 'It's all my mistake.'

'Not really, you did a right thing,' told his father. 'Because yesterday it rained for almost two hours; you can't wait that long in a store.'

'But now, because of my running in the rain, I have got cold and fever.'

'True. That's what you should remember in future. As it is the rainy season, always carry a small umbrella in your school bag, or borrow one from your teacher or friends if the sky looks like it would rain.'

Just compare this with Rishi's approach. Both are advising Mohan, but Rishi talks about what he didn't do, Mohan's father concentrates on what needs to be done in future.

Not only that, in the discussion that Mohan is having with his father, he is actively involved. His father makes him think and analyse what has happened, and then gently suggests what he should do in future.

Everyone does not act mature, be it adults or children. We should understand that advice is not welcome in most of the places, and we would change our approach to make it a two way talk, exactly like how Mohan's father did.

Sometimes, you may want others' support for your own benefit. In such scenarios, there is every possibility that they may assume you are just using them, and they may raise a question 'what's in it for me?' Now, if they start thinking about their benefits, it can turn into an ugly conversation. Instead, you can be proactive and bring that topic in advance. For example, 'I have an examination next week. If you teach me how to solve these problems, it would of great help to me. At the same time, it can be a good practice for your own exams later.'

Again, notice how it becomes a mutually understanding talk. When you talk about the benefits, people will like you, and support you. They will be genuinely happy when you win, because of two reasons – they know they have helped you succeed, and there is something in it for them too.

If you remember this two-way example, you can turn any relationship into a goldmine. Just focus on a collaborative discussion, mutual respect and sharing of benefits, everything else would follow automatically!

Who Runs Your Show?

In your school, you can notice two kinds of kids – controllers and followers. Notice that I haven't used the term 'leaders' here. If you find a group of 100 people, may be one or two of them would emerge as leaders, But almost 50% of the group would be controllers or influencers. Such people, young or old, are able to influence others just like a remote control that decides what a television set should do.

Followers are the other set of people who get influenced by the controllers. They may be doing this because of various reasons – love, fear, respect, trust, or plain lack of self confidence. Whatever may be the reason, a controller–follower relationship is not healthy in the long term. It may work for a few days or weeks; but after that it will start going downhill.

This is because dependency in a relationship is a very sensitive matter. Few people may like the influence exerted by others on them, and sometimes benefit from it. But the general observation is that most people don't prefer it. If a relationship tries to erode their personal space, they will simply try to get away with it instead of continuing.

So, there are two kinds of possibilities: Others influencing us, or we trying to influence others. In both ways, it leads to a bad relationship. We should strive to avoid this at all costs. The trick is to know how much of dependency is allowed, or is healthy in a relationship.

When two people interact, they are not just talking about their own worlds. Knowingly or unknowingly, they try to intrude into the other person's space, like two intersecting circles. It is natural in any relationship, and it would benefit both the parties involved, as long as it doesn't become too much like stepping on each other's foot.

But how much is too much? How do we know when to stop? First, always remember the personal space. Each one of your friends, or other relationships have this preference, some would like you to come forward and support them even in their most personal decisions, whereas others would prefer to keep those for themselves. Hence, it is important for us to closely observe and know who stands where – this is similar to the self-control scale we saw earlier.

Once we know how much of an influence/control the other person is comfortable with, we should change our behaviour accordingly. As an example, for somebody who doesn't like others controlling them, you may want to stay away from giving your advice on matters concerned to him/her, and refrain from making suggestions. This will make sure that you are not entering into the personal territory/space of the other person.

Similarly, when others are trying to influence you, there is a magical formula you should remember: Always take advice and suggestions from others, but let the final decision be yours!

This simple formula ensures that you don't spoil your relationships by saying, 'I don't want your advice.' But at the same time, you are not letting others control you. So, you would be able to hear from many people what they think about a particular issue, carefully weigh the options you have and make the final decision. As you are not being influenced by others beyond asking for their suggestions, the success or failure of the decision falls totally on you, which is good.

The main reason for adopting this formula is, when you are listening to many people, you are bound to hear many views, which may be contradicting. One person may say something which is totally different from what the other says. If you allow them to influence you, it will look like you are being pulled from opposite directions.

Remember, it is very difficult to please everyone. If you try to do it, you are actually not pleasing anyone.

Once upon a time, a man and his son were riding a horse. It was a sunny day and both of them were very thirsty. When they stopped for water, a villager asked them, 'Why are you treating that horse cruelly? It's too hot today and how can that poor creature carry both of you?'

The man thought he was right, and so, got down and started walking. Now, only his son was riding the horse.

After a few miles, another passerby came along. When he looked at this strange group, he started advising,

'The boy is very young; he can walk. But you are older and look more tired, why don't you ride the horse and ask your son to walk?'

It made sense. So the man and his son switched places. They walked on for some more time, until another passerby cursed them, 'Don't you have any love for your son? How can you make him walk in this hot sand, while you enjoy your ride?'

Now, the man was frustrated. He also got down from the horse and both of them started walking.

A small boy looked at this, and started laughing aloud, 'When there is a horse, why don't you ride on it? Why are you walking alongside the horse?'

This is what happens when we try to please everyone. At the end of the day, we will be the loser.

Another common mistake people do is, try and satisfy others at the loss of their own interests. This doesn't mean we have to be selfish. But we shouldn't be stupid to let another person run our show, or steal it to run their show.

When Mahatma Gandhi was a young school boy, one of his friends was heavily influencing him. He advised him, 'You need to eat meat to become stronger like me.' Gandhi listened to him for few days. After that his own conscience told him what he was doing was wrong, and he went his way. After that he never touched meat.

Building and maintaining good relationships is essential. But at the same time, we need to keep the control of our life in our hands!

Five Stages of a Relationship

There is a very famous saying, 'Rome was not built in a day!' This means, the great city of Rome didn't appear overnight, it was not developed by few people in a short span of time. Instead, many generations worked on it continuously, and this huge city and civilization was built bit by bit.

Our interpersonal relationships are also a lot like Rome. They are not built in a day or two; but go through certain changes over a period of time, which we can clearly observe. A famous psychologist George Levinger has proposed a model, which identifies five stages in any relationship. They are:

- Acquaintance
- Buildup

- Continuation

- Deterioration

- Termination

It is not necessary that each relationship goes through all these five stages. Some of them may cover only four, or three of them. But in general, you can observe the trend in any relationship.

To understand George Levinger's model, let us analyse these five stages with an example.

Arjun was in a birthday party, where a friend introduced him to Rohan. They just exchanged a "Hi" and agreed to meet later.

This is the typical first stage in any relationship, getting acquainted with somebody. Depending on how frequently Arjun and Rohan meet, and how much their interests match, they may move from acquaintance to the next stage. Otherwise, many relationships break at this stage itself, just because both the parties involved don't see any need to continue further.

In our example, Arjun and Rohan met regularly. They discussed about their studies, hobbies, favourite movies, sports and many more. Slowly, they started enjoying each others' company. A mutual trust builds between them, together they start doing many adjustments we have seen in this book so far.

This second stage is called buildup. This cannot continue forever because, the next stage (continuation) requires lot of commitment from both the people involved. If that is missing, then once again the relationship may go back to the first stage, or break forever.

Continuation means, the two friends (Arjun and Rohan) agree mutually that both of them want to continue this friendship. They may not say it in words but in actions. It will slowly become very clear to them if they are going to remain friends, or split.

At this stage, there are some very important factors like continuing trust, flexibility and non-stop development of relationship. It takes time to get into, and maintain this stage of any relationship. But they are the people with whom we would spend (or would like to spend) the maximum time. If you observe carefully, almost all your good friends will be in this stage.

Now, the fourth stage is a little painful. Arjun and Rohan may remain good friends forever, and skip these last two steps altogether. But not all relationships are like that. Especially, relationships which are built on self interest, or made because of fear, or some other forced reason, tend to deteriorate after some time. For example, if Arjun and Rohan became friends just to study together for an examination, the need for them to be together vanishes soon after the exams are over. Both of them would start thinking, 'Why should I hang around with this guy?'

This fourth stage, deterioration, is very dangerous and a definite relationship killer. Sometimes, due to various circumstances, some of your good relationships may enter this trap. If you are careful, you can notice and prevent it from failing forever.

But how can we spot the deterioration stage in a relationship? It's rather simple. It will usually start with some boredom, conflicts of opinion. If both the parties take these arguments very personally, lot of heated debates may follow, each person would try to do something to displease the other, just to make them upset.

This will lead to communication gap. Knowingly or unknowingly, both the people would try to avoid the other person, or tell them very few things, hiding their real feelings. This affects the mutual trust they had once upon a time, leading to a relationship disaster.

Of course, these are all ugly. We don't want any of our relationships to go this way. So, pay careful attention to these symptoms. When you see these with any of your friends or other acquaintances, have an open talk with them and analyse what's going wrong. This simple discussion might help you patch up with your deteriorating relationship and you may save it.

If you are not able to, or don't want to do it for some reason, you will be staring at the fifth and final stage in interpersonal relationships – termination. This is where the involved people (Arjun and Rohan) decide to part explicitly, or are forced to split due to other circumstances.

For example, Arjun's father may move to a new city, and they may lose touch because of this distance. In such a scenario, they don't have to terminate their relationships but continue their communication via phone, email etc. In that case, they may go back to acquaintance or buildup stages again, and have a lifelong friendship!

As we saw earlier, all relationships needn't go through these five stages necessarily. But we have to be aware of these stages, and continuously try to analyse if we want to move up, or avoid a slide down.

It takes many years to grow a mighty tree. But a single axe may kill it in a matter of hours. Let's make sure it doesn't happen to our dear relationships!

Ready, Steady, Praise!

Once, a great speaker came to our office. He delivered a wonderful session on anger management and we were very pleased to hear such brilliant techniques from an expert like him.

After the session, I had a chance to meet him personally, and congratulated him for the excellent lecture, 'You must be delivering such sessions almost every day. How do you motivate yourself to do well again and again, without getting tired?'

He smiled and responded, 'When I speak, I can see the audience in front of my eyes. The satisfaction in those faces, their smiles, applause, everything acts as an immediate praise for my work, which keeps me charged up to do well every time I give a lecture.'

If experts like him are in need of such praise for continuous motivation, what about you and me? Praise is the easiest (and cheapest) gift you can give anyone. Whether it is a small kid doodling his first drawing, or a music wizard composing a symphony, everyone secretly long for praise. In fact, that may be one of the primary reasons they do their work so well. When a well deserved praise is given at the right moment, it pumps them up.

So, naturally, praise is an important ingredient in the recipe for successful relationships. If you use it well, it will transform you into a magnet that attracts people in no time. This doesn't mean you have to praise everything that people do. Instead, you need to become good at spotting praise-worthy moments from everyday life.

For example, you are late for school, and in a hurry to catch the school bus. Your little brother helps you by bringing your shoes and socks. That's sweet of him, isn't it? If yes, why don't you tell it to him immediately? There is no point in waiting till the evening, or till his next birthday to praise him. So, deliver the praise as soon as the praise-worthy deed is completed, and people would love it.

Management expert Ken Blanchard has a very interesting name for this technique - "Catching People

Doing Right". Normally, people love catching others doing wrong things, so that they can criticise them. But when the same people do something right, people don't praise them. This is a double edged sword – nobody notices when you are right 100 times, but make a small mistake, everyone jumps at you. Won't you hate it?

This is what happens in many classrooms. Teachers scold pupils for their wrong answers; but when they give a correct response, or write a beautiful essay, no one cares to praise them. To build successful relationships, you need to move away from this habit of looking for people's mistakes. Instead, focus on catching people doing right things. Whenever they do, praise immediately!

Oliver Wendell Holmes once described relationships as "The Pleasing Game of interchanging praise." Mutual praise will enhance the experience and support both the parties involved to grow and improve. In history, praise has changed many lives. As an example, let me tell you the story of a small boy, whose fortunes improved because of a single praise.

This young boy was working in a London store as an assistant. It was hard work, extending into many hours everyday. He was struggling constantly to get the approval of his boss. But however hard he tried, nobody praised him for anything.

After many months, one fine day he decided, 'Enough of this, I can't take it any longer, I am going to quit.'

But there was a problem. His family was very poor, and they needed his salary to make their ends meet. If he stopped working, they all would go hungry. The boy understood the situation, and decided to make a sacrifice for his family. He silently hid all his emotions and continued in his horrible job, even though he didn't enjoy it.

One day, he wrote a letter to his old teacher, explaining all his problems. He told openly, 'I don't feel like living anymore.'

The teacher was very upset to read his letter and wrote back to him immediately, 'Son, I know you are very clever. I can very well understand your current problems and frustrations. But you should not worry too much about them, as they will vanish soon. Don't lose hope. You are born to achieve great heights. Your intelligence and hard work will help you on this superb journey.'

This small praise motivated that London boy a lot. He started focusing on the big picture and concentrated on his hobbies of reading and writing. Later, he became one of the greatest novelists in English literary history, H. G. Wells!

If an one page letter can make an upset boy into a great writer, just think of all the changes your praise could make in this world. Never underestimate the power of praise.

Basically, praise is a way of saying you care. So, it shouldn't stop with mere words, your actions should match with what you are saying. A boy runs to his friend and shows his school report excitedly, 'Hi friend, guess what, I have passed my examinations with distinction.'

His friend is very busy playing a video game. Without looking at him he simply says, 'Well done pal!'

This is praise. But is it genuine? It's very obvious that the other friend is occupied with something else and merely uses some nice words to praise the boy — his excitement is not explicit. This kind of fake praise may de-motivate the boy instead of encouraging him.

So, when you are praising someone, make sure it's not incomplete or shallow in nature. For this, you need to make few of these things clear, in proper words:

- Whether what they did was right?

- Why do you think it deserves praise? How do you feel about their achievement?

- Do you find anything lacking in them? Is there something they need to improve? Can you help them improve? If yes, how?

For Example, 'Ravi, I am very happy that you have passed your exams with flying colours. Last month, you were struggling with the same subjects, and teachers gave you a study schedule and an improvement plan. Normally, in such situations, people take a negative stand and get into a worry loop. But you were different, you took it as a challenge, worked hard, improved constantly and you have got excellent marks now. Well done!'

This sounds good. But it shouldn't go above the head for Ravi. While we should keep our praise liberal, we also need to give them positive criticism on areas of improvement, and how we can support them.

Again, let's go back to Ravi. 'Pal, I am thrilled to see your exam results. But remember, compared to other subjects, you have scored less in mathematics. I guess you need to work harder on this for your next examination. Let me know how I can help you on this!'

You can even go one step further, 'I know a friend who is an expert in teaching math. Tomorrow I will introduce you to him; I am sure he would be of great help to you.'

This completes the loop beautifully. We are not only praising Ravi for what he has done, we show genuine care by pointing to the improvement areas, giving suggestions, and offering to help. It's the best part in all relationships.

One problem is that some people may not take criticism positively. They may want to hear only good things about themselves. When others say bad things, or pinpoint their mistakes, instead of improving in those areas, they start hating the people who did so.

To avoid such problems, you need to learn the art of sugar-coating your messages. In earlier days, when people fell ill, the medicines prescribed to them were very bitter. Most of the patients refused to swallow or drink their medicines.

To solve the problem, ancient doctors introduced a very simple solution. They hid a tablet inside a banana or a sweet, and served it to the ill people. Those patients, without knowing what is inside the fruit, or the sweet, ate it cheerfully, and that improved their health.

Remember, you need to adopt sugar coating very carefully, and use it only when you are really interested in improving the other person's shortcomings. Otherwise, it may be seen as a misuse or manipulation, which is bad for your relationship.

Words are very powerful. Especially, when used for praising somebody, they magically bind many relationships together. Just make sure you use them intelligently!

Honesty In Relationships

There was a small boy in a village. He was very mischievous and was always looking forward to tease and make fun of others. His favorite prank was, running around the village shouting 'tiger, tiger'. When he did that, everyone was afraid and ran to the shelter. Some even started crying out of fear.

After a few minutes, the boy came back laughing hysterically. In reality, there was no tiger at all. The innocent villagers fell for his mean trick. As this happened regularly, people learnt their lessons and started ignoring the boy. Even if he would cry 'dinosaurs' no one cared!

One day, the boy was working in the nearby forest. A tiger actually came and started chasing him. He ran for his dear life. When he reached the village, he started shouting desperately, 'Help, Help, I am chased by a tiger.' Obviously, the villagers were very well aware of this prank and didn't believe the boy. They went about doing their regular chores. Nobody came forward to help him. But when they saw the tiger, they realised that the boy was right, and helped him by giving him shelter in a house. Thus his life was saved.

After the tiger went back to the jungle, the boy came out of that house. He had learnt his lesson. Cheating others may be fun, but honesty is the best policy. If that is missing, you lose your reputation, and sometimes your own life! Being honest is a minimum requirement when you have a relationship with anyone. Nobody wants to relate to a person who says something and acts in some other way.

Remember the trust factor we were discussing earlier? This is heavily dependent on how honest you are, when talking or transacting with others. If you don't stand by your words, or do something unexpected out of a relationship, that binding will not last for long.

Few kids are playing cricket together. As they have only one bat and ball, every kid gets to play exactly 10 shots, and then should hand over the bat to the next one. But one boy thought he was smart, and decided to cheat his playmates. After completing his quota of 10 balls, he said, 'I have only faced 8 balls, you need to bowl me two more.'

His friends believed him first time, and then a second time. But when this happened on a regular basis, they doubted him and allotted somebody else to do the scoring. As his dishonesty was uncovered, he had to hang his head in shame and return home.

This is just a small example. In real life, you will get many such opportunities to be honest, or to cheat others. If you are honest, naturally your relationships will be stronger, and the opposite also holds true.

Here are some ground rules for being honest with your friends and in other kinds of relationships:

Rule One: Always say what you can, don't promise too much and create unrealistic expectations. For example, instead of 'I will make you an expert at chess' you may want to say 'I will help you on the basics of chess, the rest will come with practice. We can do it together'.

Rule Two: Try to avoid telling lies. When you speak the truth, you don't have to really remember anything, instead if you hide things from people, the pressure of remembering what you said to whom will literally break you. Sometimes, the lie may be useful to the other person in some way. For example, telling your injured friend, 'It's not very big, you will be able to start playing pretty soon' may be a lie. But that will give him hope and help him feel better. Except in such situations, don't resort to telling lies.

Rule Three: When you have two relationships, never compromise one for another. You may have best friends and others, but explicitly treating them differently will make one happy, and hurt the other. For example, your teacher asks all the students to sit in pairs for some exercise. You want to group with your best friend Roshini, but your bench mate doesn't want to part with you.

Now, if you want to be honest, you need to tell the truth, 'Sorry friend, I want to sit with Roshini.'

But do you know how your bench mate will interpret it? 'I don't want to sit with you.' Even though you didn't exactly use those words, that's how it will be interpreted. Compromising one relationship for another is always painful. After the exercise, when you return to your bench, you can already see some change in your bench mate's behaviour because she is hurt.

It's not easy. Balancing different kinds of relationships and making sure that everyone feels important is a very difficult task. But it is one of the essential elements in the social relationships' spectrum. If we don't do it well, we will have few good friends, and lots of haters. That won't be fun!

That's when Rule Four comes handy. Try to spend quality time with all your relationships. If it means spending an entire afternoon with a not-very-close friend, instead of your best pal, you need to take the plunge. Later, you can always go back to your best friends as the mutual trust and understanding is stronger there!

Finally, Rule Five. Never talk bad behind someone's back. That way, you are being dishonest to the relationship, to the person, and are also harming others who are listening to you. If you don't like something, tell it openly. If it requires a sugar coating, you can do it, to give the person the bitter medicine. But there is no point in going to someone else and complaining, 'I don't like what she did.'

Relationships are not a miracle, where a tree grows overnight. It takes time, lot of care, efforts and patience for you to build a relationship tree. If you want strong roots of trust in that tree, you need to make sure the plant is watered regularly with honesty. It's not a one-day affair, but a life-long commitment!

History says people who managed to make their relationship network bigger always achieved the greatest of things. It makes lot more sense in today's modern society, where the whole world has shrunk like a small village. The more the people you know in this village, the more the chances of your success.

In a nutshell, relationships are good, beneficial and essential for everyone. But they can never be built or maintained with our efforts alone. The key to success is to be honest, genuine, open and willing to respect and embrace others' opinion(s), and learn the art of inviting and involving everyone to do their bit. When healthy relationships flourish, the whole world will be a better place to live in!

www.ingramcontent.com/pod-product-compliance
Lightning Source LLC
LaVergne TN
LVHW091602180726
843489LV00014B/1111